EYE ON THE SKY

WHEN FLOODS FLOW

Gareth Stevens PUBLISHING

BY BARBARA LINDE

Please visit our website, www.garethstevens.com. For a free color catalog of all our high-quality books, call toll free 1-800-542-2595 or fax 1-877-542-2596.

Library of Congress Cataloging-in-Publication Data

Linde, Barbara M.
When floods flow / by Barbara M. Linde.
p. cm. — (Eye on the sky)
Includes index.
ISBN 978-1-4824-2880-3 (pbk.)
ISBN 978-1-4824-2881-0 (6 pack)
ISBN 978-1-4824-2882-7 (library binding)
1. Floods — Juvenile literature. I. Linde, Barbara M. II. Title.
GB1399.L56 2016
551.48'9—d23

Published in 2016 by
Gareth Stevens Publishing
111 East 14th Street, Suite 349
New York, NY 10003

Designer: Laura Bowen
Editor: Kristen Rajczak

Photo credits: Cover, p. 1 Oli Scarff/Getty Images News/Getty Images; cover, pp. 1–32 (series art) Nik Merkulov/Shutterstock.com; p. 5 Mirvav/Shutterstock.com; pp. 7 (main), 29 Anadolu Agency/Getty Images; pp. 7 (inset), 11 (inset) Malachy666/Shutterstock.com; p. 9 Konstantin Komarov/Shutterstock.com; p. 11 (main) Mario Tama/Getty Images News/Getty Images; p. 13 David McNew/Getty Images News/Getty Images; p. 15 Joe Raedle/Getty Images News/Getty Images; p. 17 Qfl247/Wikimedia Commons; p. 19 (main) Michael Nevins/US Army Corps of Engineers/Wikimedia Commons; p. 20 John Tlumacki/The Boston Globe/Getty Images; p. 21 (main) Keystone-France/Gamma-Keystone/Getty Images; p. 21 (inset) Stock Montage/Archive Photos/Getty Images; p. 22 Pixsooz/Shutterstock.com; p. 23 ronfromyork/Shutterstock.com; p. 25 Area 52 Advertising Inc/Moment Mobile/Getty Images; p. 26 Scott Olson/Getty Images News/Getty Images; p. 27 Debra L Rothenberg/Getty Images News/Getty Images.

Printed in the United States of America

CPSIA compliance information: Batch #CS15GS: For further information contact Gareth Stevens, New York, New York at 1-800-542-2595.

CONTENTS

Words in the glossary appear in **bold** type the first time they are used in the text.

DANGER: FLOOD!

Imagine this. It's been raining steadily for 3 days. The ground is completely **saturated**. When you walk on it, it feels spongy, and you sink in. Huge puddles line the streets. Nearby, the river has risen almost to the top of its banks.

As the downpour continues the next day, the situation gets worse. Your street starts to look like a lake. You see on the television that the river has overrun its banks, spreading through the nearby neighborhoods. Your area is experiencing one of the world's worst natural **disasters**—a flood!

WATCHES AND WARNINGS

The US National Oceanic and Atmospheric Administration (NOAA) issues flood watches and warnings. A flood watch lets people know that a flood might happen soon in their area and they should be careful. A flood warning means that a flood is about to start or has already started. People need to move to higher ground immediately.

Floods are the most common weather-related natural disasters. They can occur quickly or over the course of many hours or days.

WHAT IS A FLOOD?

A flood occurs when water flows onto land that's usually dry. Any amount of water from just a few inches to several feet can be considered a flood. Floods can happen anywhere in the world at any time. Most occur in an area that's near a body of water.

Floods can cause great amounts of damage, or harm. Powerful water can rip a house loose from its base, uproot trees, and drag cars and trucks around like they're toys. Raging waters also destroy crops and crumble city streets. Sadly, floods also cause loss of life for people and animals alike.

DANGERS FROM FLOODS

Floodwaters mean many dangers to people and animals. Here are some of the most serious ones:

- death or injury
- contaminated, or polluted, drinking water
- illness-carrying mosquitoes and other insects
- waste spills
- waterline or gas-line breaks and spills

FREQUENCY OF FLOOD EVENTS BY COUNTY: 1996–2013

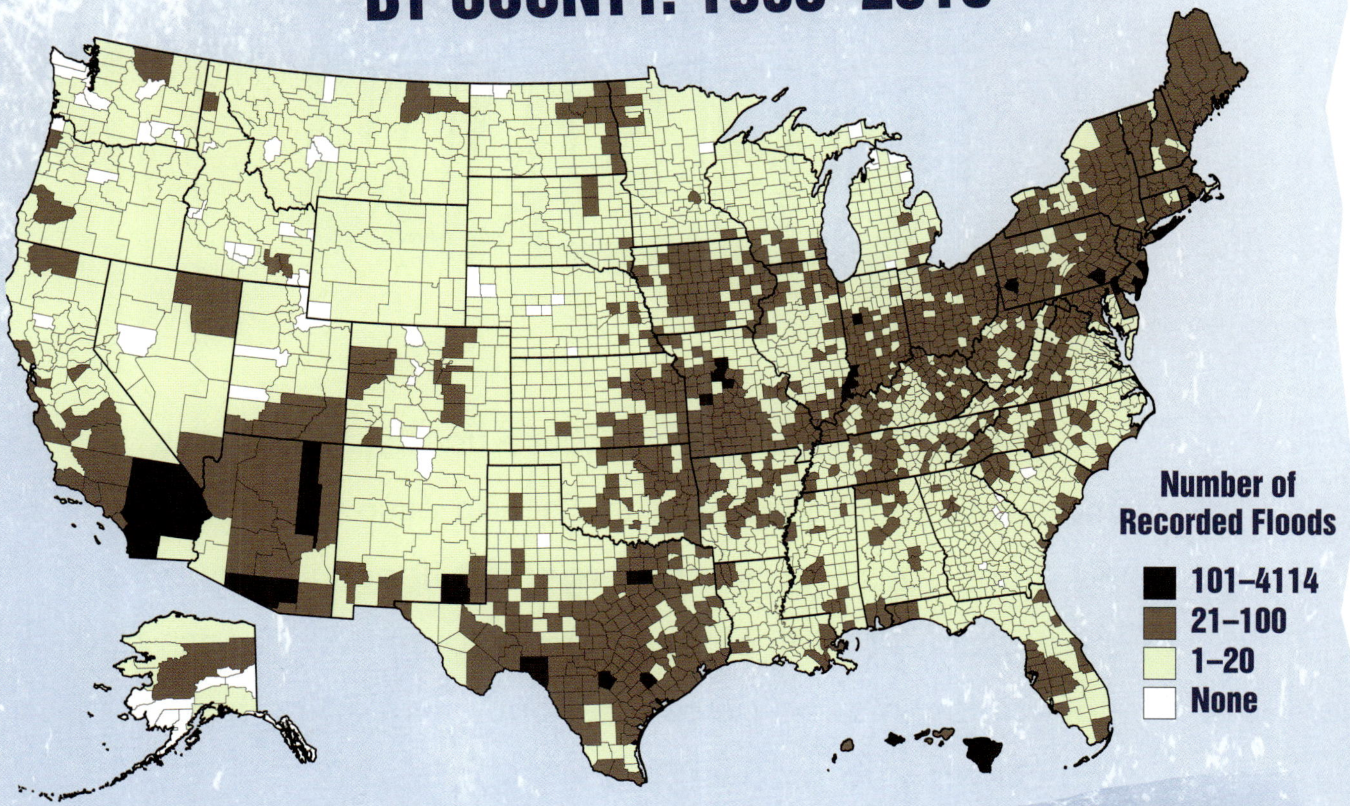

This map shows the number of floods that occurred in each county of the United States between 1996 and 2013.

A PUSHY OCEAN

Several weather events cause floods. **Hurricanes** and heavy rainstorms near the ocean push waves onto the shore, causing a **storm surge** that floods the low-lying coast. Picture a wall of water crashing onto the beach and then rapidly moving across the land, swallowing houses and chewing up roadways.

If high tide happens at the same time as the storm, more water flows ashore, creating a fiercer flood. It can be anywhere from a few feet to 20 feet (6.1 m) deep—or more. And when all that water flows back out to sea, it takes a lot of **debris** with it.

NOR'EASTERS

A nor'easter is a huge, fierce storm that forms near the Middle Atlantic or New England coast and then moves inland. Its trademarks are howling winds and driving rain and snow. A nor'easter often stretches for 1,000 miles (1,610 km) or more and lasts for several days. Floods occur along the coast.

More people die because of flooding in the United States each year than those who die from the funnel cloud and rotating winds of tornadoes, lightning strikes, or hurricanes.

RAGING RIVERS

A storm along a river can dump lots of rain, causing the river to overflow. A large river often has tributaries, or smaller rivers that run into it. When these have too much water, the volume flowing into the main river increases. The river rises over its banks, covering the **floodplains**, and sometimes going further inland.

If a river flows through a narrow valley, there's nowhere for the water to go but downstream. A river that starts at the top of a high mountain may flood areas below as gravity pulls water downward.

THE GREAT MISSISSIPPI FLOOD OF 1927

After months of heavy rain, the Mississippi River overflowed in April 1927. Over 23,000 square miles (59,570 sq km) of land flooded. Part of the reason the flood was so widespread was that the river's tributaries flooded as well. The water was 30 feet (9 m) deep in some places. This flood is still one of the worst in US history.

This map shows the Mississippi River system. It's made up of the Mississippi River and all its tributaries. This river system has a long history of many disastrous floods.

FIRE AND SNOW

Believe it or not, wildfires often can cause floods. The fire destroys trees and bushes, leaving large areas of open ground. The burnt ground can't absorb, or take in, much water, increasing the chances of floods and mudslides. The western states of California, Colorado, Oregon, and Washington are among those most at risk for floods from wildfires because of the huge fires that occur in those places.

Snowmelt from mountains often causes floods, too. When the snow melts quickly, all the icy water rushes down the mountainside, flooding the valley below. If the ground is still frozen, it can't absorb the water.

WILDFIRES AND FLOODS IN BOULDER, COLORADO

In the early 2000s, several wildfires erupted in the mountains around Boulder, Colorado. The fires left acres and acres of scarred, empty land. Then, in 2013, a severe storm soaked the area with almost 10 inches (25 cm) of rain in a little over 24 hours. Floods raced down the mountainsides, causing destruction and killing two people.

This image shows the buildup of rain into a flood in Southern California after a dry spell and wildfires in 2014.

CLIMATE CHANGE

How does **climate change** affect flooding? It's one cause of dangerous weather, such as heavier rains and stronger hurricanes. Climate change causes Earth's temperatures to rise, and warm air holds more moisture, resulting in more rain and snow. Many scientists believe that as climate change continues, storms will get even worse. Floods may become more frequent and more powerful.

Climate change is also causing sea levels to rise. Land near the ocean floods more often. Some of the land will be permanently covered by water. Large cities along the coasts will be affected. They might lose waterfront buildings and ports.

FLOATING HOUSES

About one-third of the Netherlands is at sea level or below sea level, making rising seas a real problem. However, the Dutch have begun building houses that float! These houses are anchored to the land, but also have supports that let them move up and down with the sea level.

Rising temperatures on Earth are causing the ice at the North and South Poles to melt, which is causing ocean levels to rise. Cities like Miami, Florida (shown here), that are found on the ocean are expected to see a rise in floods.

FLASH FLOODS

Some floods build up over time, but others, called flash floods, happen quickly. Suppose snowmelt or heavy rains pound down on a frozen river. The force of the water breaks the ice into chunks. These chunks may jam and block water from flowing. With nowhere else to go, the river water will overflow its banks and flood surrounding areas.

Big cities are at risk for flash floods. Storm drains can fill up and overflow onto the streets, which have no way to absorb the water. Highway underpasses, underground garages, and subway lines can be dangerous places during a flash flood.

THE MOST DISASTROUS DISASTER

Floods and flash floods cause more damage in the United States than any other weather disasters each year—about $5 billion. About 90 percent of all natural disasters declared by the US president include flooding. Flash floods are the most destructive. Almost half of deaths during a flash flood occur in cars and trucks being driven through waters.

Dry riverbeds called arroyos (uh-ROY-ohz) fill with water during different seasons. However, a flash flood has overwhelmed this arroyo in the Gobi Desert with water. This often happens to arroyos in the southwestern United States.

LEVEES AND DAMS

For thousands of years, people have been building structures to control water. A levee is made of earth or cement and is designed to hold back the water. It runs parallel, or along the sides of, the body of water. Levees are built high enough to protect an area from a certain amount of water. But a levee can overflow or even break.

A dam is built across a river and has strong gates to control the water's flow. Water behind the dam builds up into a lake. Heavy rains, floods, or earthquakes can weaken a dam and cause it to burst. This creates a flash flood downriver.

A NEW ORLEANS CATASTROPHE

On average, New Orleans lies about 6 feet (1.8 m) below sea level and is almost completely surrounded by water, which is held back by levees. In 2005, Hurricane Katrina pounded the area with rain. The levees on Lake Pontchartrain and the Mississippi River gave way, flooding almost the entire city. Thousands of people lost their homes. More than 1,800 died.

This illustration shows the structure of a levee, simply. The freeboard is extra height added to the levee in case flood levels reach even higher than those the levee was meant for.

FORECASTING

Today, there are scientists who study the weather. They're called meteorologists. They want to be better able to forecast, or predict, when floods and flash floods might occur. They're also trying to figure out how to make the effects less deadly.

Radar and weather **satellites** are used to track storms and weather conditions in order to predict rain events. They create computer-generated models of rivers to see what might happen.

Meteorologists are always looking for new ways to predict floods. One project asks people to download an app onto their cell phones that tells scientists about local floods. Another project trains citizens to safely spot and report flash floods.

Meteorologists use computers to predict floods—but some happen too quickly to truly predict.

JOHNSTOWN FLOOD

Not long ago, there were few ways to tell if a flood would occur. In 1889, a dam broke near the town of Johnston, Pennsylvania. While it had been raining for days, there was no way to know the conditions were bad enough to cause a flood. More than 2,200 people died. Another major flood, shown in the image below, occurred in Johnstown in 1936.

FRANK LESLIE'S ILLUSTRATED NEWSPAPER

JOHNSTOWN

No. 1760.—Vol. LXVIII.] NEW YORK.—FOR THE WEEK ENDING JUNE 8, 1889. [Price, 10 Cents.

PENNSYLVANIA.—THE APPALLING DISASTER AT JOHNSTOWN.—ENORMOUS DESTRUCTION OF LIFE AND PROPERTY BY A FLOOD FROM THE MOUNTAINS.—SCENE BELOW THE DEVASTATED TOWN.—[See Page 311.]

BEFORE A FLOOD

Before a flood starts, the best thing to do is get out of the area. Listen for news reports about **evacuation** procedures. If you can't get out, then move quickly to the highest ground possible. Go upstairs or even onto the roof of a house. If your house only has one story, then get up on a table or a countertop. Make sure your pets are safe. Move other belongings to higher levels.

If you're outside, find a dry hillside. Climb a tree if you have to, but be aware that rushing waters can uproot even large trees.

MAKE A FLOOD KIT

Your flood kit should include the following items:

- waterproof bags
- drinking water
- canned or dried food
- money
- medicine and first aid items
- clothing
- batteries, flashlights, and radio
- important papers

Sandbags piled against a door can help keep out floodwaters.

DURING A FLOOD

Never walk through a flooded area. A person walking can get swept away or knocked over by a mere 6 inches (15 cm) of rushing water and even drown.

Don't drive on a flooded street, because you can't see how deep the water is—and you don't know the condition of the road. It only takes 2 feet (0.6 m) of water (about up to your knees) to carry a car away.

Do your best to stay calm. Listen to reports on an NOAA radio, a TV, or a mobile device. Stay in touch with others in your neighborhood if possible.

EVACUATING

If you have to evacuate because of a flood, unplug all electrical devices in your home. Turn off the water and gas to the house. Empty the refrigerator and leave the door open (to prevent it from floating away). Pack some clothes and food in waterproof bags. Then follow the directions of the emergency rescue workers.

In December 2014, heavy rain caused flooding across Southern California. Flooded streets are unsafe to drive on!

AFTER A FLOOD

The floodwaters may have **receded**, but that doesn't mean it's safe to return home. Disaster crews need to go into the area first to check for fallen power lines, broken pipes, downed trees, or other problems. Whole sections of streets may have been ripped up, leaving huge holes.

A building might look okay on the outside, but there may be inside damage that makes it unsafe. A flood usually leaves a lot of mud and debris. If water seeps into walls, the walls will have to be repaired or replaced. People who return to their home after a flood face a long, tiring cleanup job.

SAVING YOUR PETS

Sometimes people have to leave their pets behind during a flood or pets get separated from their owners. Animal rescue teams go into flooded areas to rescue pets and take them to shelters. The National Guard, firefighters, and other groups also help. Many people are then reunited with their pets after the flood is over.

The rain, wind, and flooding caused by Hurricane Sandy destroyed houses along the New Jersey shore in 2012.

FLOOD BENEFITS

Floods cause great harm, but they also have some benefits. When a river overflows, it leaves a mixture of soil, debris, and other matter on the land. It also carries some of this mixture to other areas along the course of the river. This mix often helps plants grow well. In many areas, farmers are happy to see the floods come. A flood may help get rid of sick or weak plants, leaving room for stronger, healthier ones to grow.

Don't forget that a flood is part of nature's **cycle**. And nature's cycle will keep on going!

FLOOD SAFETY FOR SPIDERS

The country of Pakistan had a severe flood in 2010. About 20 million people were affected by the great amount of rain that fell. So were millions of spiders! They climbed trees to escape from the floodwaters. They wrapped the trees in cocoons and stayed there for several months until the floodwaters receded.

Rivers in Turkey flooded after days of heavy rain in December 2014. The streets were nearly impassable.

GLOSSARY

climate change: long-term change in Earth's climate, caused partly by human activities

cycle: a sequence of events that repeats

debris: the remains of something that has been broken

disaster: an event that causes much suffering or loss

evacuation: the act of leaving an area because of danger

floodplain: flat land next to a river that often floods

hurricane: a powerful storm that forms over water and causes heavy rainfall and high winds

radar: a machine that uses radio waves to locate and identify objects

recede: to go down or to become less

satellite: an object that circles Earth in order to collect and send information or aid in communication

saturated: full of water

storm surge: a rise in the level of water along a coast caused by rain

FOR MORE INFORMATION

BOOKS

Mason, Paul. *Floods.* Mankato, MN: Smart Apple Media, 2012.

Meyer, Susan. *Adapting to Flooding and Rising Sea Levels.* New York, NY: Rosen Central, 2013.

WEBSITES

Floods
www.ready.gov/kids/know-the-facts/floods
Learn the facts about floods, and make a family disaster plan.

Floods 101
video.nationalgeographic.com/video/101-videos/floods
Watch videos of real floods as they happened to understand their causes and destructive powers.

Rain & Floods
www.weatherwizkids.com/weather-rain.htm
Read about the causes of floods, and find out how to stay safe before, during, and after a flood.

INDEX